Praise for the Beli

"As grandparents of 50 grandchildre
Believe . . . and You're There series. Parents and grandparents, gather your children around you and discover the scriptures again as they come alive in the *Believe . . . and You're There* series."

—STEPHEN AND SANDRA COVEY
Stephen Covey is the bestselling author of *7 Habits of Highly Effective People*.

"Bravo! This series is a treasure! You pray that your children will fall in love with and get lost in the scriptures just as they are discovering the wonder of reading. This series does it. Two thumbs way, way up!"

—MACK AND REBECCA WILBERG
Mack Wilberg is the Music Director of the Mormon Tabernacle Choir.

"This series is a powerful tool for helping children learn to liken the scriptures to themselves. Helping children experience the scriptural stories from their point-of-view is genius."

—ED AND PATRICIA PINEGAR
Ed Pinegar is the bestselling author of *Raising the Bar*.

"We only wish these wonderful books had been available when we were raising our own children. How we look forward to sharing them with all our grandchildren!"

—STEPHEN AND JANET ROBINSON
Stephen Robinson is the bestselling author of *Believing Christ*.

"The *Believe . . . and You're There* series taps into the popular genre of fantasy and imagination in a wonderful way. Today's children will be drawn into the reality of events described in the scriptures. Ever true to the scriptural accounts, the authors have crafted delightful stories that will surely awaken children's vivid imaginations while teaching truths that will often sound familiar."

—TRUMAN AND ANN MADSEN

Truman Madsen is the bestselling author of *Joseph Smith, the Prophet.*

"My dad and I read *At the Miracles of Jesus* together. First I'd read a chapter, and then he would. Now we're reading the next book. He says he feels the Spirit when we read. So do I."

—CASEY J., AGE 9

"My mom likes me to read before bed. I used to hate it, but the *Believe* books make reading fun and exciting. And they make you feel good inside, too."

—KADEN T., AGE 10

"Reading the *Believe* series with my tweens and my teens has been a big spiritual boost in our home—even for me! It always leaves me peaceful and more certain about what I believe."

—GLADYS A., AGE 43

"I love how Katie, Matthew, and Peter are connected to each other and to their grandma. These stories link children to their families, their ancestors, and on to the Savior. I heartily recommend them for any child, parent, or grandparent."

—ANNE S., AGE 50

Mother of ten, grandmother of nine (and counting)

At the Miracles of Jesus

At the Miracles of Jesus

Book 2

ALICE W. JOHNSON & ALLISON H. WARNER

Salt Lake City, Utah

Text © 2008 Alice W. Johnson, Allison H. Warner
Illustrations © 2008 Jerry Harston

All rights reserved. No part of this book may be reproduced in any form or by any means without permission in writing from the publisher, Deseret Book Company, P. O. Box 30178, Salt Lake City, Utah 84130. This work is not an official publication of The Church of Jesus Christ of Latter-day Saints. The views expressed herein are the responsibility of the authors and do not necessarily represent the position of the Church or of Deseret Book Company.

This book is a work of fiction. The characters, places, and incidents in it are the product of the authors' imaginations or are represented fictitiously.

DESERET BOOK is a registered trademark of Deseret Book Company.

Visit us at DeseretBook.com

Library of Congress Cataloging-in-Publication Data

Johnson, Alice W.
Believe and you're there at the miracles of Jesus / Alice W. Johnson, Allison H. Warner ; illustrated by Jerry Harston.
p. cm.
ISBN 978-1-59038-722-1 (pbk. : alk. paper)
1. Jesus Christ—Miracles—Juvenile literature. I. Warner, Allison H. II. Harston, Jerry ill. III. Title.
BT366.3.J64 2007
232.9'55—dc22

2007005794

Printed in the United States of America
Worzalla Publishing Co., Stevens Point, WI

10 9 8 7 6 5 4 3

Believe in the wonder,
Believe if you dare,
Believe in your heart,
Just believe . . . and you're there!

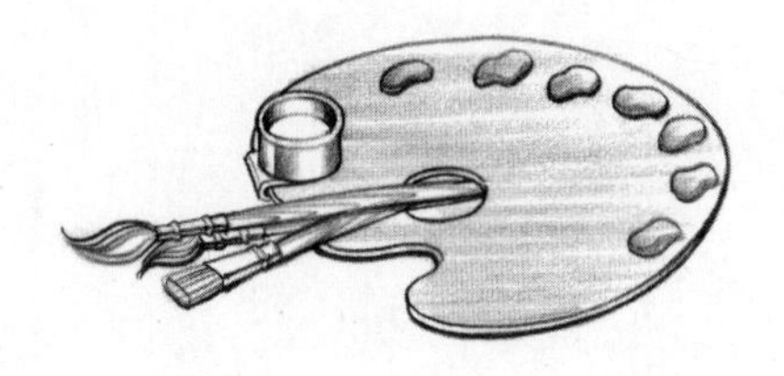

Contents

Chapter One

Matthew's Predicament

"You can't do that," Katie told her brother, sounding shocked. "That is totally cheating!"

"Not exactly," Matthew hedged.

"Well, either it is or it isn't. Which one is it?" Katie demanded.

"Hey, don't be so hard on me," Matthew protested. "Cameron's my friend, you know."

"Some friend," Katie sniffed.

Matthew and Katie stood at the door of Grandma's cottage, waiting for her to join them.

"Hi, guys!" Peter called out, bounding down the flagstone path that led to the small white building in the corner of Grandma's backyard. "Grandma's coming! What do you think she's painted for us this time?"

"I don't know and I don't care," Matthew answered sullenly. He plopped down on the front stoop of the cottage and rested his chin in his hands.

"Hey, what's the matter with you?" Peter said, surprised at his brother's reply.

Katie put her arm around Peter's shoulder. "It's hard to be nice when you're planning to do something wrong," she explained, shooting a look of contempt at Matthew.

"You're going to do something wrong, Matthew?" Peter asked in disbelief.

"Thanks a lot," said Matthew, glaring up at Katie.

Katie pursed her lips together smugly, but didn't say anything.

"What are you planning to do?" Peter asked. Matthew didn't answer. "Come on, you can tell me! I'm your brother!"

Seeing a chance to get Peter on his side,

Matthew relented. "Okay, here's the thing. You know who Cameron is, right?"

"Everybody knows who Cameron is! He's that guy who thinks he's so cool," Peter answered.

"He *is* cool!" Matthew retorted.

"If you say so," Katie muttered under her breath.

"Will you let me finish?" Matthew was getting frustrated.

"Sure," said Katie, "go ahead." She shrugged as if nothing Matthew could say would change her mind.

"Okay," Matthew began explaining to Peter. "Next week, we have a big math test at school, and it counts for a lot of our grade. Cameron is going on a vacation with his family, and he won't be here for it."

"Well, can't he make it up when he gets back?" Peter asked.

"Yeah, he can make it up," Matthew continued. "He just asked if I could write down some of the problems I remember from the test so he could have something to study from when he gets back."

Matthew tried to sound casual, as if Cameron's request were completely understandable.

"What did you tell him?" Peter asked, wide-eyed.

"I said, 'Sure, if I can remember them.'" Now Matthew shrugged, as if this were an obvious answer.

"But that's cheating!" Peter declared emphatically.

"Did Katie tell you to say that?" Matthew came right back.

"No!" Peter replied. "I figured it out all on my own."

"It doesn't take much to figure that out," Katie added.

"Come on, you guys," Matthew pleaded with them. "He's only asking for a few questions. It's not like he wants me to tell him the answers." And then Matthew added persuasively, "I'm only trying to be nice."

"Are you afraid he won't be your friend if you don't do it?" Katie asked.

"No," Matthew replied, but he didn't sound very convinced. "Why are you asking?"

Katie answered sincerely, "Because it doesn't seem like something you would do."

Matthew didn't know what to say. He felt trapped. Cameron was one of the cool guys at school, and Matthew had always wanted to hang around with him. This was just a little favor, wasn't it? Or were Katie and Peter right?

"I'm coming, darlings!" Grandma called as she closed the back door of her house and headed across thc lawn toward the cottage. "All lined up, I see. Is everyone ready?"

"We're ready!" Peter said excitedly.

"All right, who's going to start the password?" Grandma asked.

"Me!" It was Peter, as usual. Katie grinned, patted her little brother on the back, and nudged him forward.

Grandma stood at the door waiting for her grandchildren to recite the verse that would grant them entrance to the cottage.

"Believe in the wonder," Peter began.

Katie continued, "Believe if you dare."

"Believe in your heart," Matthew bellowed his line with gusto.

Grandma joined them as they all chimed, "Just believe . . . and you're there!"

Then Grandma reached into her pocket and retrieved the key to the art cottage. Unlocking the door, she opened it wide and the children hurried in.

In the corner of the cottage stood Grandma's easel. This time, it was covered with a large white sheet, concealing the new painting Grandma had promised.

The anticipation of returning to the cottage had been almost too much for the three children to bear. Ever since their first adventure traveling into one of Grandma's paintings, they had thought of little else. Was it possible that their visit to the wilderness of Judea to witness the baptism of Jesus was only something they had imagined? But it all seemed so real!

The children looked around the studio. There, on a wall near the fireplace, hung the painting of the River Jordan, which had taken them on their thrilling scripture adventure in Judea. Katie went right up to it to examine the figures. There were the tiny people on the path to the river, just as they had been before.

"Are they moving?" Matthew whispered quietly, so Grandma wouldn't hear. Katie shook her head.

"Are you sure?" Peter asked hopefully. "Not even a little tiny bit?"

"I'm sure," whispered Katie sadly.

Grandma busied herself with blankets and pillows on the floor in front of the covered easel. "Did you remember your journals?" she asked.

"I have them all right in here," Katie said, pulling them out of her backpack.

"Grandma, where are we going today?" Peter asked brightly.

"Going? We aren't *going* anywhere," Grandma replied with an innocent smile. "We're staying right here to see the painting and hear some stories from the Bible!"

But with Grandma, you never knew.

Chapter Two

At the Seashore

"Do you know the best thing about painting scripture scenes?" Grandma stood next to the easel and addressed the seated children. "It's thinking about each one of you while I'm working. For instance, I wonder which part of the story you'll think is most exciting, Peter. Katie, I try to imagine which characters will inspire you. And, Matthew, my thoughtful grandson, I always think about what important lessons you'll learn and share with the others. Oh, darlings, I've been so eager for you to see this new one!"

And with a flourish, Grandma lifted the draped

cloth, unveiling a beautiful blue seascape dotted with dozens of wooden boats. In the surrounding hills, an ancient village was nestled.

"This," Grandma announced, "is the Sea of Galilee, and a small fishing village near its shores."

"Hmmm . . . I wonder what we'll do in a fishing village?" Peter seemed to be thinking out loud.

"Who is going to be in a fishing village?" Grandma asked.

"Uh, er," Peter stammered, catching himself, "no one, I guess . . . well, just the people in the Bible story . . . of course . . ." His voice trailed off.

"Peter, why don't we just sit back and let Grandma start reading to us?" Matthew prompted Peter, giving him a look.

Peter got the idea right away. He pantomimed locking his lips with an imaginary key, crossed his arms, and settled into the pillows on the floor.

Grandma sank into her overstuffed rocking chair, picked up her scriptures, and began thumbing through the pages, looking for a good place to start. "Now," she instructed, "everyone settle back, get comfortable, and pretend that you're there."

The children sat breathless at Grandma's feet. This was the moment that would tell them if their adventure at the River Jordan was just a one-time thing or if the magic would continue. This was the moment they would finally know.

Grandma began reading, "And the same day, when the even was come, [Jesus] saith unto them, 'Let us pass over unto the other side.' And when they had sent away the multitude, they took him even as he was in the ship."

Katie and the boys strained to detect the slightest movement anywhere in the painted landscape, hoping with all their might that this painting would be like the last one; but the water stayed motionless and the trees remained still. Katie's heart began to sink. A look of disappointment washed over the two boys.

"And there were also with him other little ships," Grandma went on.

And then . . ."Oooh." A little gasp escaped Peter's lips. He pointed to a group of boats. Matthew grabbed Peter's hand and put it back in his lap. But Grandma read on, seeming not to notice.

Katie saw it next. It was unmistakable! One of the small fishing boats in the harbor was bobbing gently on the water!

Looking at Matthew and Katie, Peter mouthed with exaggerated lip movements, "LET'S GO!"

"Shall we?" Katie whispered to Matthew.

"Okay, but not through the water," he whispered back. "We don't want to land on one of those fishing boats. We'd have a hard time explaining that one!"

"How about right here?" Impulsive Peter pushed his finger right into the seashore. First his finger vanished, and then his whole hand disappeared. And he kept right on pushing! With not a moment to spare, Katie grabbed hold of his other hand and lunged for Matthew. Holding hands, the three children were suddenly engulfed by a giant "schlooping" sound, and, together, they were sucked right into Grandma's painting!

Just like before, they felt themselves carried away—away from the time they knew so well, away from Grandma's steady voice, away from the safe, warm cottage.

"It's happening again! I can't believe it!" Peter

called out to the others as the air around them roiled.

"Well, believe if you dare! And hold on tight!" Katie urged her brothers, her blonde ponytail streaming behind her in the wind.

"We're in for another adventure!" Matthew squeezed his eyes shut tight.

Then the swirling air began to subside, and the three children felt the rocky seashore beneath their feet. Matthew slowly opened his eyes. There stood Peter and Katie, wearing draped tunics and open sandals, just like before!

"Thank goodness we're in these clothes again." Matthew sounded relieved.

"I'm kind of starting to like them," said Peter, admiring his robes.

"Yeah, Matthew," Katie teased. "If only cool Cameron could see you now!" Matthew ignored Katie's remark.

The children looked up and down the shore, trying to figure out exactly where they were in the painting. The water stretched out in front of them, with the soft blue sky arching above the low hills that rimmed the sea. Small, flat-roofed houses were nestled in the surrounding hillsides. Here and there, people made their way to and from the seaside.

Not far from the children, a group of fishermen sat, inspecting their large, coarsely tied fishing nets. They could be heard talking and laughing as they worked.

"Hey, let's go over and ask those fishermen what they're doing!" Peter suggested with his usual enthusiasm.

"Hold on just a minute." Matthew grabbed Peter's arm before he could run off. "I think we should think carefully about what we say and who we say it to, don't you?"

"Good idea!" agreed Katie. She loved Peter's outgoing and exuberant nature, but thank goodness for Matthew's caution! "Look at all those people walking to the shore. I wonder what's going on over there," she said, deliberately shifting Peter's interest.

Peter and Matthew looked along the shoreline to see a large group of people clustered around a man. They pressed in around Him as He slowly made His way to the edge of the sea.

"I'm going to see what's happening," Peter called out as he headed toward the group. "Don't worry, I won't talk to anyone!"

Matthew and Katie looked at each other, laughing. "Well, let's get going," Katie grinned, shaking her head. "Who knows what trouble he could make!"

Chapter Three

Candlesticks and Bushel Baskets

Peter skirted the crowd, pausing every few feet to hop off the ground, trying to get a good look at the man in the center. Matthew and Katie finally caught up with him. "What's going on?" Matthew asked, trying to catch his breath.

"I can't tell yet. No one will let me see," Peter replied. Deciding to take a different approach, he dropped to his hands and knees and crawled between the onlookers. "I'll be right back," he called as he disappeared into the crowd.

"Who is the man in the middle of all these

people?" Matthew asked, standing on his tiptoes, straining to see.

"There's only one person I can think of who would attract such a crowd," Katie answered.

"Do you really think it could be Him?" Matthew asked.

A murmur rippled through the crowd as people whispered to one another, "He is going to teach!" One by one, the people sat down on the shore, and the view in front of Katie and Matthew cleared. There, standing before the seated people was the man they had seen on another shore—the shore of the River Jordan. It was Jesus, the Savior of the world.

"Katie, it's Him," Matthew whispered, suddenly overcome with the same feelings of joy and awe that had filled him once before.

"I know," Katie answered softly.

Peter came into view, making his way through the seated multitude. He looked awestruck at the scene unfolding before him.

"Could you hear what He was saying?" Matthew asked.

"Not really. When I got up there, a nice man

asked everyone to sit down. He said Jesus is going to stand in that boat right there so everyone can hear Him teach." Peter pointed to a small boat anchored close to the shore.

"Let's listen," Katie said as Peter sat down beside her. "We don't want to miss anything."

And in a voice pure and gentle, Jesus spoke.

"Ye are the salt of the earth: but if the salt have lost its savour, wherewith shall it be salted? it is thenceforth good for nothing, but to be cast out, and to be trodden under foot of men."

A man seated near the children leaned over to his wife and said, "That is what He taught on the mountain. Do you remember when I told you about it?"

"Yes," she nodded. "But what does it mean?"

"Well, salt is a very important ingredient. We put it in most foods because it helps food stay fresh and makes it taste better."

Before the man could go on, Jesus continued. "Ye are the light of the world. A city that is set on an hill cannot be hid. Neither do men light a candle, and put it under a bushel, but on a candlestick; and it giveth light unto all that are in the house. Let your light so shine among men, that they may see your good works, and glorify your Father which is in heaven."

Katie turned to her brothers, "I think I know what He means. If we do good things, others will see how wonderful the gospel is."

"That means that all of our choices matter, doesn't it?" Matthew sounded serious.

"Exactly," Katie gave her brother a gentle smile, full of meaning.

Jesus went on, but Matthew seemed lost in his own thoughts. As a follower of Christ, he ought to be an example to his friends. If he did wrong things, it would be like hiding his light under a bushel. But if he let his light shine forth, his friends might not think he was a candlestick—they might think he was just an old stick in the mud instead! Matthew's thoughts were churning.

Now the sun was high in the sky and very, very hot. Many in the crowd shielded their eyes, while others pulled their head scarves lower on their foreheads. The disciples began walking through the multitude, telling the people that it was time for Jesus to rest.

"Come again later in the day when the sun is lower in the sky," they instructed.

People in the crowd stood up. They all looked as if they had somewhere to go. "What should we do now?" Katie wondered aloud.

"I don't know, but I sure could use some lunch!" Peter said, listening to his stomach growl.

"Let's follow all these people. It looks like they're headed for the village. Maybe we can find some food there." Matthew tried to sound hopeful.

"We could offer to do some jobs in exchange for food if all else fails," Katie said bravely, but secretly she was worried.

"Great idea! Let's go!" As usual, Peter led the way with confidence.

Encouraged by Peter's positive outlook, Matthew and Katie fell in step, and the threesome marched toward the village.

"Katie, Matthew, Peter!"

All three children stopped dead in their tracks. Someone was calling them by name!

Katie's heart was beating so hard she could hear it in her ears. Who could possibly know their names? Nobody even knew they were here!

Slowly, Matthew reached out and took Katie by the hand. Now, if only he could reach Peter's, they could make a quick escape back to Grandma's cottage. But Peter was nowhere in sight.

"Katie, Matthew, Peter!" their names rang out loudly again. Almost frozen with fear, Katie and Matthew slowly turned to see who was calling their names.

Chapter Four

A Happy Reunion

Once they turned around, Matthew and Katie were startled to see that a boy was running toward them, calling out, waving wildly. To their amazement, they recognized him. It was Jesse, their friend from their last visit to Palestine! Peter was already running toward Jesse and had almost reached him.

Hugely relieved, Katie and Matthew also headed to the happy reunion.

"Jesse! I never thought we would see you again!" Katie cried. She was elated to see their friend. "What a wonderful surprise!"

"Where did you go so quickly last time? We looked all over for you, but you were nowhere to be found," Jesse chided.

Thankfully, before Katie could answer, Abigail and Seth appeared. "I knew it was you!" Abigail squealed excitedly.

Katie reached up to hug Abigail, who was riding on her father's back. Katie had wondered many times how little Abigail, whose legs were paralyzed, was doing.

"Oh, Abigail! You are still your happy self, I see. I don't think I would be so cheerful if I couldn't walk," Katie said.

"Yes, you would," Abigail assured her. "There is always so much to be grateful for. How about my father getting baptized? That blessing alone will keep me thanking God for the rest of my life!"

"I guess you could be right." Katie still sounded doubtful.

"I am certain of it," Abigail smiled. "Are you here for long, Katie?"

"Not really. Probably just a day or two," she answered.

"This time, you must be sure to tell us when

you leave so that we can say a proper good-bye," Abigail insisted.

"Why are you here?" Matthew asked Jesse. "Do you live in this village?"

"No," replied Jesse. "My grandfather lives here. We heard that Jesus was teaching, so we came for a visit."

Seth explained more. "My father is a fisherman. He makes his living here on the Sea of Galilee. We are planning to get on his boat to get closer to Jesus."

"A boat!" Peter exclaimed "Wow! Can I come?"

"We would love to have you all come with us," Seth responded, tousling Peter's mop of curly hair. "But first we are going to eat our noonday supper at my father's fishing hut. Will you join us?"

"Thank you," Katie replied gratefully. "We would love that." And the children followed Seth and Abigail toward a cluster of small shelters.

"Where is your grandfather?" Matthew asked Jesse. "Isn't he coming with us?"

"He fished all night, so he is asleep right now," Jesse explained.

"He fishes at night?" Matthew questioned.

"You do not know much about fishing, do you?" Jesse kidded his friend.

"Not very much," Matthew answered, embarrassed by his lack of knowledge.

"Actually, I did not know much either," Jesse confessed, "until my grandfather taught me. Here on the Galilee, many people fish at night and sleep during the day."

"Here we are," Seth announced as they arrived at one of the small wooden shacks. All around, enormous nets were laid out on rocks to dry. Small fish were spread over wooden racks, drying in the hot sun.

"Oh, boy, what is that smell?" Peter asked, pulling his robes up over his nose. "That is disgusting!"

Seth threw back his head and laughed. "It takes some getting used to, doesn't it?"

"I'd say," Peter answered, his face all screwed up.

"These fish have been salted, and when they are dried, they will be sold in cities like Damascus and Jerusalem," Seth explained. "That is how my father earns money."

"Well, I don't think he is going to make much money trying to sell *these* fish," Peter declared, holding his nose.

"You'd be surprised," Seth replied. "I'll let you try some for lunch."

"No, thanks," Peter said with a shudder. "I think I'll stick to some bread."

"Okay, Peter," Seth said with a chuckle. "Come, let us eat." All the children gathered around as Seth distributed bread, cheese, and sweet, chewy figs. When they had finished eating, he passed around a leather sack filled with cool water. The children drank thirstily, then headed toward the boat.

On their way, Seth waved to two men sitting beside another fishing hut. "Come meet some fisherman friends of mine," he invited the children.

When they were near, Seth made the introductions. "Nahum and Daniel, meet our friends, Katie, Matthew, and Peter."

"Katie." One of the men repeated her name thoughtfully. "That is an unusual name."

"I'm named after my grandmother," Katie explained.

"Ah." The other man nodded his approval. "Then your parents named you well."

"What are you doing?" Matthew asked Nahum and Daniel.

"I am mending our net. If it has holes, it could tear and let the fish out," Nahum explained. "Daniel is attaching weights around the outside of the net. That way, when we throw it out into the water, the weights sink down and trap the fish underneath the net."

"What do you do with them after you catch them?" Katie asked the men.

"Oh, we have very strict rules about fishing. Any fish that doesn't have scales is thrown away. It is considered unclean, and no proper Jew would eat unclean food."

"Who made that strange rule?" Peter looked puzzled.

Abigail was surprised. "Why, Moses, of course! Certainly you know about the law of Moses!"

"Oh, sure we do." Matthew came to Peter's rescue. "So, what do you do with the fish that have scales?" Matthew asked, trying to change the subject.

"Well," explained Nahum patiently, "first, we roll them in salt to preserve them and so that they will taste good. Then we dry them and sell them to merchants who take them to market."

"And don't forget the taxes." The other fisherman, Daniel, gave Seth a look of annoyance. "We have to pay a tax for every fish we catch."

"I do not take taxes from you," Seth protested.

"Only because we live in different villages," Nahum pointed out. "You collect taxes from all the fishermen in *your* town. If we didn't have to pay taxes, fishermen could make a decent living. But as it is . . ."

Without warning, Daniel started singing, and after just a few words, Nahum joined in. Half laughing, half singing, the two of them sang with gusto:

We fish all night, and work all day
To keep the hunger pangs away.
But here is a disturbing fact:
The Romans then demand a tax!
The publicans say, "If you please,
We'll squeeze you 'til you almost bleed."

And just when you're about to cry
They'll ask for more—'til you're bone dry.
Then off the top they always snitch
A bit to keep—that's why they're rich!
With no remorse and no regret
They happily live off our sweat!

Then, even more raucously and loud, they swayed back and forth as they finished off with a rousing chorus:

A publican, a publican!
We see him coming, and we run!
Quick, hide your shekels or, good grief,
He'll take them all, the dirty thief!

Seth had no answer for the unkind song. He tried to laugh and shrug it off, but inside he couldn't help feeling wounded. Yes, paying taxes was very difficult for fishermen. But collecting them was Seth's job!

Ever since he had been baptized, Seth had been trying to justify his work as a publican, but it was getting harder as each day went by. He quietly sat for a few minutes, lost in his worries.

"Father, Father," Jesse came running, "Jesus is ready to teach again. Can we take grandfather's boat out in the water to listen to Him now?"

"Yes, son," Seth answered. "Come, we will all go."

"Abigail," Peter said, "Matthew and I will carry you down to the boat."

Abigail beamed at his suggestion. "I feel like a queen when you carry me between you," she said.

Peter and Matthew linked their arms. "Your throne is ready, your majesty." They bowed as Katie helped Abigail up. And laughing as they went, the happy children made their way down to the water's edge to board the boat.

Chapter Five

The Queen and Her Court

Now the sun was lower in the sky, and its rays danced along the water's surface, glinting and flashing in a magical display of sun and sea. Dozens of people were moving toward the shore, making their way to the place where Jesus was preparing to teach.

Seth jumped into the water and waded out to retrieve one of the larger boats. Dragging it behind him, he brought it into the shallow waters.

"The queen and her lady-in-waiting will sit here in the middle of the boat," he said, bowing low with a flourish. The girls giggled and nodded their approval. Once they were seated, Seth instructed, "Peter, sit up front and be our lookout. Jesse and Matthew, you can each take an oar, and I'll sit in the back to steer."

"Ah, phooey!" Peter was disappointed. "I wanted to row."

"All right," Matthew said agreeably. "You row, and I'll be the lookout. How does that sound?"

"Great! Thanks, Matthew!" Peter put both thumbs in the air. "You're the best!"

The children took their places in the old and creaky wooden vessel. Katie looked at the wet floorboards nervously. Could this boat really keep them afloat? But before she could voice her fears, Peter began paddling furiously with his oar, and the boat began spinning around in circles.

"Hold on there a minute, Peter!" Seth cried out, half laughing. "We are going to have to work as a team, or we are not going to get anywhere. Let's try rowing together. Ready? Row . . . row . . . row," he called out in rhythm.

With a little effort, Jesse and Peter synchronized their strokes, and Seth steered from the back as the

boat cut through the water toward the spot where Jesus was teaching.

It was early spring, and swallows flitted silently above the surface of the lake under the late afternoon sky. The surrounding hills were blanketed with a new growth of grass and patches of colorful wildflowers.

"Father, look! There He is!" Abigail's eyes lit up as they approached the boat in which the Savior stood.

As they drew closer, Jesus' voice became louder. "Whereunto shall we liken the kingdom of God?" they heard Him say, "or with what comparison shall we compare it? It is like a grain of mustard seed, which, when it is sown in the earth, is less than all the seeds that be in the earth: But when it is sown, it groweth up, and becometh greater than all herbs, and shooteth out great branches; so that the fowls of the air may lodge under the shadow of it."

"Last time, He compared us to the salt of the earth," Matthew observed. "He likes comparisons, I guess."

"There is always so much to learn from His teachings," Seth responded. "The more you think about them, the more important truths you discover. I have been thinking about the salt. I think Jesus wants us to mix in with other people, the way salt mixes into bread. Just a little salt can change the flavor of a whole loaf. And if we obey Him, we will make everything happier wherever we go, too."

"That's right," said Katie thoughtfully. "I remember when He said that if salt has lost its savor, it's not worth much. But good salt makes everything taste better."

"I want to be like good salt in the world." Abigail sounded determined.

"I think you already are." Katie squeezed her shoulder. "You've made my life happier; that's for sure."

Jesus made a few more comparisons and then sat down in the boat. The children heard Him say to His disciples, "Let us go over unto the other side of the lake."

The disciples sent the multitude away and began rowing their boat out into the sea.

"Can we follow them?" Abigail asked her father.

"The journey across is too long, I think. We need to get the boat back to Grandfather before dark," he answered.

"Could we go just a little way?" Jesse sounded hopeful. "There is still a lot of light, and it is such a beautiful evening."

"Yes, right now it is beautiful. But storms can come up very quickly when the winds sweep down the ravines between those hills," Seth explained as he surveyed the horizon. But the sky was clear, the breeze was soft, and five hopeful children were looking at him with pleading eyes.

"All right," he relented. "We can go a short distance. But we will have to turn back in just a few minutes. Agreed?"

"Agreed!" five happy voices shouted in unison.

And Peter and Jesse, with Matthew as lookout, began rowing out into the vast, watery expanse.

Chapter Six

A Sudden Storm

Seth tightened his grip on the rudder as the breeze picked up, urging the old fishing boat on its way. Now the people on the shore could hardly be seen, as the boat carried its passengers out onto the sea. Katie and Abigail sat contentedly in the middle of the boat, loving the fact that they were being treated like royalty.

The sun moved a little lower in the sky, and looking about, Matthew sighed with rapture, "It's too beautiful for words, isn't it?"

"It is," Abigail agreed.

Just then, Seth said, "Oh-oh." He sounded

concerned. "Let's start back toward shore," he instructed the boys as a strong gust of wind ruffled his robes.

"Father, what is it?" Jesse asked.

Seth pointed to a bank of heavy grey clouds that had suddenly appeared on the horizon. "I do not like the look of those clouds," he said, trying not to sound alarmed.

The wind that had been helping them along now blew against them as they rowed back toward shore. Their progress was slow, and the sky grew blacker and more hostile with each passing minute.

Seth strained to steady the rudder against the waves, which rolled higher and higher. "Matthew!" He had to holler to be heard. "Help Peter row!" Matthew scrambled to help Peter manage his oar while the wind churned around them.

A ferocious gust brought a wild wave crashing over the side of the boat, dumping several inches of water into its bottom. "Oh, Father, there is water in the boat," Abigail cried, "and I cannot swim!"

Katie could see the fear in her eyes. She put her

arms around Abigail's small body and held her tight, trying to keep her still and dry.

"Abigail, I can swim. I'll hang on to you," Katie offered bravely. She hoped Abigail wouldn't sense the panic that was beginning to grip her heart.

Katie looked over at Peter. Now his thin arms were being whipped around by his oar, but he seemed determined to hang on. Jesse looked frightened, but

he, too, clung to his oar, courageously battling the fierce waves.

"Matthew, we must get rid of this water in the boat! Jesse and Peter, you keep rowing!" Seth shouted instructions to the boys.

Matthew grabbed a woven basket at his feet and began scooping up water and dumping it overboard. It seeped out the sides of the basket, and

Matthew had to work fast, so that it didn't all go right back into the boat. Abigail and Katie used their hands to scoop out as much water as they could. Katie wasn't sure they were much help, but at least it gave them something to think about besides the raging water that threatened to sink them.

"I think we're making progress," Matthew shouted to Seth. At that very moment, a massive wave caught him from behind, knocking him off his feet and sweeping him over the side of the boat. Everyone screamed in horror as Matthew disappeared beneath the angry water.

"Matthew, Matthew!" Peter shrieked into the wind, scanning the waves for his brother. But he was nowhere to be seen.

Katie's heart was pounding. In desperation, she uttered a silent prayer for Matthew's safety. Just then, on Jesse's side of the boat, Matthew appeared, tossed up from beneath the waves, his arms flailing in desperation. He gulped in a big breath of air and started swimming toward the boat with all his might.

Jesse hollered, "Matthew, take hold of my oar and I will pull you in!"

Matthew reached for the oar as a wave crashed over his head, sucking him away from the boat, leaving the oar just beyond his grasping fingers. He disappeared again under the water, but surfaced again after a moment. This time, Jesse leaned out farther over the side of the boat and Seth lunged across the boat for Jesse's feet, holding on with all his strength.

"Come on, Matthew, you can do it," Seth called, encouraging Matthew as he struggled to reach the oar. And then, without warning, the wind seemed to pause, as if it were catching its breath. Matthew made one last frantic stroke, and his hand caught hold of the wooden oar!

Jesse pulled the oar inward, Matthew clinging with both hands to its end. Seth stood ready, and when Matthew was within reach, he leaned forward, wrapping his strong arms around the half-drowned boy. With one heave, he hoisted Matthew over the side of the boat and gently laid him in its bottom.

There Matthew lay, sputtering and coughing,

completely bewildered by the ferocity of the storm that had swept him overboard so quickly. But he was equally bewildered by the sudden calm all around them now, as the boat gently rocked him, back and forth, back and forth.

Chapter Seven

Hard Decisions

"If you had told me this morning how my day would end up, I wouldn't have believed you," Matthew declared as he emerged from the hut, where he had put on some dry robes.

"I think that is true for all of us," Seth agreed.

"How *did* this day start anyway?" Peter asked, trying to recall.

"Remember?" Abigail asked. "I saw you on the shore, and we all went to hear Jesus teach."

The events of the day flooded back into Matthew's mind. He remembered Jesus' words and the fishermen drying their catch. Oh, yes, the fishermen. Matthew recalled the unkind things they had said to Seth about collecting taxes and the taunting song they had sung. Most of all, he remembered the sadness that had settled on Seth's face.

"You seemed upset by Nahum and Daniel earlier," Matthew said softly to Seth.

Seth lowered his head and nodded. "I find myself in a very hard position," he confided. "I must make a living for my family, and collecting taxes has been my profession. It has supported us well, but the people I collect from don't want to have anything to do with me."

"Do you *have* to collect more than the Romans require?" Matthew asked him.

"Well, I suppose I don't *have* to, but then I would make no money at all for my work. How would we live?"

"I see your dilemma," Matthew said, thinking about his own problem back home with Cameron.

"Since I have been baptized, it has been harder," Seth went on. "I am a follower of Jesus now, and I should bring light to people, not make trouble for them."

"Yeah," Matthew agreed. "But sometimes, it seems easier to hide your candle under a bushel, doesn't it? Like when a friend wants you to do wrong things."

"Hmmm," Seth looked at Matthew thoughtfully. "It sounds as though I am not the only one with a problem, my boy."

"No, you aren't," Matthew replied, slowly shaking his head.

"And it has to do with a friend, I take it," Seth continued to probe.

Matthew nodded, looking down at the ground.

With a motion toward the fishing boat, Seth announced to the other children, "Matthew and I are going to check the boat and see if it is ready to be taken fishing tonight. We will be back shortly."

Seth and Matthew walked along the shore. The sun hung low in the sky, and it cast a faint glow across the calm sea. There wasn't a hint of the storm that had raged just a short time before.

"Well, Matthew, just what is the dilemma you are facing?" Seth asked when they were alone. "I can see from your face that it troubles you."

"One of my friends wants me to help him. But Katie and Peter think that what he wants me to do would be cheating."

"Oh, I see," Seth said. "Do *you* think it would be cheating?"

"Not really," replied Matthew.

"Are you sure?" asked Seth, looking into Matthew's eyes.

Matthew looked away. "No, I'm not sure at all," he finally admitted.

"That is what I thought," replied Seth with a knowing smile on his face.

"But I don't want to lose a friend," Matthew protested.

"I know just how you feel," Seth explained. "Many of my best friends are publicans, too. All of them take much more money from people than I do, and they say I make them look bad. They want me to demand more, like they do."

"What did you tell them?" Matthew asked, hoping for an easy answer.

"I have not yet told them what I will do. But they are starting to insist that I make a choice," he said.

Seth and Matthew walked silently along the shore, each thinking about his difficult situation. Matthew spotted a small, purplish stone in his path, and he glumly kicked it along in front of him as he walked. Finally Seth asked, "What are we going to do, Matthew?"

"It shouldn't be this hard to decide, should it?" Matthew said. And then he added, "Especially since we have promised to follow the teachings of Jesus."

"Yes, and today on the boat, He said we should let our lights shine, so that other people could see our good works," Seth remembered. "Matthew, I think you and I are hiding our lights under a bushel basket."

"I don't have a bushel basket," Matthew kidded.

"I do not have one, either," Seth laughed. "I mean that we know in our hearts what is right. That is the light of Jesus Christ. But we are more worried about what our friends think than we are about letting our light shine forth."

"Maybe so," Matthew mused. "Maybe so." And he picked up the purple rock, dropping it into the small pocket sewn onto his tunic just below the waist.

Just then the sound of girlish giggling interrupted their conversation. Seth and Matthew looked up to discover a parade making its way along the shore. Katie led the way, with Peter and Jesse following behind. Between them, they carried Queen Abigail, who laughed with delight as she basked in the glow of the setting sun.

Her head was adorned with a crown fashioned from fishing ropes, and draped around her neck was a necklace made of wildflowers. Katie playfully waved a fan of leaves over Abigail's head as they made their way.

"It looks like we're going to have some visitors," Seth observed, smiling at the sight of the happy children.

"Father," Abigail cried. "Here you are. We have been having so much fun! It is such a lovely evening with the light shining across the water. Isn't it beautiful?"

"Yes, it is beautiful," he said, lifting his smiling daughter into his arms. He gazed out at the shimmering water. "It is always beautiful to see the light shine, isn't it, Matthew?"

Chapter Eight

"Only Believe"

"Children! Children, wake up," Seth urged, shaking them gently.

"What is it, Father?" Jesse asked, shielding his eyes from the glare of the sun, which had risen. It flooded onto the roof of his grandfather's house, where Seth and the children had spent the night.

"Jesus has returned. Look, you can see His boat out in the water." Seth pointed to the small ship they had seen leaving just yesterday.

Peter, now fully awake, jumped up and leaned over the edge of the roof, scanning the water for the boat. "There it is! I see it, I see it," he cried excitedly. "And people are already gathering to hear Him!"

Abigail called upward from the door of the house, "Are you all ready?"

"We're coming," the three children called back, descending a ladder to the courtyard below.

Abigail sat perched on Seth's back with her arms wrapped tightly around his neck. He slid his arms under her thin legs to support her, and together they led the group toward the sea.

About then, the boat carrying the Savior reached the shore. As He got out, a man ran toward Him, falling at His feet.

They could hear him pleading, "My little daughter lies at the point of death: I pray thee, come and lay thy hands on her, that she may be healed; and she shall live."

"Isn't that Jairus?" someone in the crowd asked.

"Yes, he is one of the rulers in the synagogue. And yet he comes to Jesus to heal his daughter!" marveled another.

Jesus turned toward the village, following Jairus to the place his daughter lay dying. The crowd moved right along with Him.

"Is Jesus really going to heal her?" Abigail asked Seth as they walked with the multitude.

"Perhaps, Abigail. Perhaps He will." Seth sounded unconvinced.

"I believe He will!" Abigail exclaimed, her voice filled with conviction and hope.

Seth couldn't bring himself to answer. He heard the hope in Abigail's voice, and he would have given anything for his daughter to be healed. But her legs had been crippled since birth. Could such a miracle be possible?

"Excuse me, I must get to Jesus," a woman said as she pressed from behind Seth and Abigail. "I know that if I can only touch His robes, I will be healed."

The crowd parted slightly, allowing the woman to approach Jesus from behind as He walked with Jairus. When she was near, she fell on one knee, reaching out to touch the hem of His robe for a brief moment. And as her fingers connected, she felt her sick body become well and strong.

Abruptly, Jesus stopped and turned around. Searching the multitude, He asked gently, "Who touched my clothes?"

"Master," one of His disciples said, "there are so many people thronging around you, many of them have touched you."

But Jesus slowly surveyed the crowd, His eyes searching. The woman, now afraid and trembling, stepped forward and fell down before Jesus.

"I have suffered with a sickness for twelve years. I have been to many doctors and have spent all my money. But I did not get better. I knew if I could but touch thy clothes, I would be healed," she said, still fearful but full of faith. "And I was, Master. I am healed."

With kindness in His eyes and tenderness in His voice, Jesus spoke to her, "Daughter, thy faith hath made thee whole; go in peace."

Then He turned again toward Jairus's house as the woman watched Him go, her face shining with gratitude and wonder.

"Jairus, Jairus," someone cried out, bursting through the crowd. It was one of Jairus's servants. "You do not need to trouble the Master any further," he wept. "Your daughter is dead."

But Jesus turned to Jairus and counseled him lovingly, "Be not afraid, only believe."

Instructing everyone else to stay behind, Jesus entered the house, taking with him three of his disciples, Peter, James, and John, along with the grief-stricken father of the girl.

"Oh, Father, Jesus is going to give life to Jairus's daughter again," Abigail said, sounding certain that He could. Certain that He *would.*

Fear and doubt crept back into Seth's heart. "What if—" he started to say, but then the strength of Jesus' words pierced his troubled heart: *Be not afraid, only believe.*

That is it, Seth realized. *I have been afraid. I have been afraid to follow Jesus completely. I have been afraid to really believe His promises.*

"What if, what?" Abigail asked him, interrupting his thoughts.

"Nothing," Seth replied. "I was—" but before he could finish his sentence, a young girl came running from Jairus's house.

"She lives, she lives!" she exclaimed as she rushed toward the waiting crowd.

"What? Tell us what happened! Is it true?" the onlookers questioned in disbelief.

The girl began, "When Jesus came in, He said,

'Why make ye this ado, and weep? The damsel is not dead, but sleepeth.' Many of the people there laughed and told Him that He was wrong, that she was indeed dead."

"What did He do then?" someone asked.

"He sent them all away and took only Jairus and his wife to their daughter's bedside," she continued, breathless with astonishment. "We all waited in the courtyard for a few minutes. And then, through the window, we saw Jairus's daughter walking around in the house! *Walking around!* That is when I came to tell you what happened."

The news swept through the crowd. The little girl who had been dead was alive! Seth and the children hugged each other joyfully. And Abigail, still riding on Seth's back, pressed her face against his ear and whispered, "Do you see why I believe, Father?"

Seth, his eyes full of tears and his voice full of love, whispered back, "Yes, darling, I see."

Chapter Nine

Because of His Love

"Put me down, Father," Abigail said. Seth and Abigail were making their way along the road away from Jairus's house.

"Right here in the road?" he asked.

"Yes, I want to be here where I can touch Jesus when He walks by," she explained.

"Are you sure He will come this way?" Seth asked.

"I am certain of it." She smiled up at her father.

"Well, the others are ahead of us now. We were all going back to Grandfather's hut by the shore."

Seth strained to see the other children ahead in the crowd, but he couldn't pick them out.

"Don't worry, Father," Abigail reassured Seth. "Jesus will be along soon, and then we can catch up with the others at the hut."

Seth saw the desire in her eyes. He knew now that Jesus had great power. Why, He had even raised the dead! But Abigail was counting on a miracle. *Please don't let my sweet angel be disappointed,* he silently prayed.

He and Abigail moved to the front of the crowd lining the road. There, they discovered many other ailing people who were waiting like Abigail, hoping to be healed. There was a blind man, a boy who shook with palsy, and others who couldn't walk, each eagerly peering down the road, each full of anticipation and hope.

Suddenly, a hush came over the multitude as Jesus and His disciples emerged from Jairus's house and paused at the gates of the courtyard. Then they began slowly walking along the road, approaching the spot where Seth and Abigail sat.

Now is the time, Seth thought. *Now is the time*

to stop being afraid that Abigail will not be healed. Have faith, he told himself. *Have faith!*

"He is coming closer, Father," Abigail cried, as Jesus came within reach.

She leaned forward, trying to touch His robes, but they were just beyond her grasp. Jesus kept making His way forward. He would be lost in the throng if they didn't move quickly. *Have faith,* Seth reminded himself.

Pushing all doubt from his mind, he scooped Abigail up in his arms and hurried ahead, farther down the street. Once again, Abigail waited for Jesus to pass. This time, Seth grabbed Abigail's hand, interlocking his fingers with hers. At the right moment, they reached together for the hem of Jesus' robe.

Their hands lingered only for a moment, but in that moment, a powerful sensation filled Seth's body with love and joy. So strong was the feeling, that Seth knew he would never be the same. Overcome, he knelt next to Abigail in the road still clutching her hand in his.

She tugged gently at his fingers. Looking into her eyes, Seth saw that she had experienced the same glorious feeling. Gratefully, she laid her head on his knee, and he gently stroked her hair.

The hush that had fallen when Jesus passed by was now replaced by gasps of surprise and delight. "My eyes, they see now," the blind man exclaimed.

"The palsy has disappeared," cried a mother, marveling at her son standing straight and tall.

Abigail looked at her father, her whole face shining bright with certainty and happiness.

"Steady me, Father," she said, clutching Seth's arm. Slowly, but with perfect faith, she pulled herself up, until she was eye to eye with her kneeling father. Her legs felt strong and firm under her.

Carefully, she lifted one foot off the ground, placing it in front of the other. Then she lifted her other foot. And then, step by timid step, Abigail was walking!

Seth could not contain his excitement. He reached down and, wrapping his arms around his beloved daughter, he lifted her up and turned her around and around in the road.

"Father! Abigail!" It was Jesse, leading the other children back toward Jairus's house, looking for his father and his sister. "Where have you been?"

"We were right here, weren't we, Abigail?" Seth laughed, his tears blurring his vision. Gently, he put Abigail down on both feet.

"Father, what are you doing?" Jesse lunged forward, reaching to steady his sister. "Abigail will fall!"

But smiling, Abigail walked to Jesse, throwing her arms around her big brother.

Matthew stood looking on. "It's a miracle!" he declared, his voice choked with emotion.

With tears coursing down his cheeks, Jesse asked, "What happened, Father?"

"She was sure that Jesus could heal her," Seth said reverently. "We knelt together at the edge of the road and waited for Him to pass by."

"I touched His robe, and I was healed," Abigail finished the story. "And so were many others."

"Oh, Abigail. It's all because of your faith!" Katie said, filled with awe and admiration.

"No, Katie," Abigail gently corrected her. "It is all because of His love."

Chapter Ten

Choosing Light, Choosing Right

Joyfully, Seth and the children walked back to Grandfather's fishing hut. There, they sat down to eat a simple noonday supper together and marvel over the events of the day.

As they talked, Nahum and Daniel appeared. "We have been told that this Jesus of Nazareth performed many miracles in the village this morning," Daniel began. "Have you heard?"

"We didn't just hear about them," Jesse replied with an enormous grin. "Look!" And on cue, Abigail stood up and walked toward the men.

"It . . . it cannot be," an astonished Nahum

sputtered. "This girl was crippled from birth! Who is this man called Jesus?"

"He is a mighty miracle worker and a great teacher," Seth explained. "Many even believe He is the Messiah."

"We heard that He just went to Bethsaida by boat. We were thinking of rowing over to hear Him," Nahum said. "But now that I have witnessed what He can do, I most certainly want to see this man for myself."

"I feel the same, Nahum. Let us go now," said Daniel. Then he turned to Seth and the children, "Would you like to go with us in our boat?"

"Oh, how I would love to hear Jesus teach one more time before we leave!" Matthew spoke his heart without thinking.

"You're leaving?" Jesse asked, disappointment written on his face.

"Yes," answered Katie. "We must return soon to our father and mother. The place we live is far from here."

"Well, don't forget to say good-bye this time!" Abigail reminded them.

And with that, Seth stood and said, "Well,

Nahum and Daniel, if you'll ride with a publican, we would all love to join you."

"Oh, no, folks," Peter piped up. "I'm not getting on a boat again, no sir! That last trip was enough for me!"

Katie, too, was nervous, looking over the water and surveying the sky.

"It looks better today," Jesse reassured them, "and besides, we will stay close to shore if we are just going to Bethsaida."

So the group, anxious to hear the Savior again, hurried to the water's edge and began wading out toward the boat.

Abigail splashed and giggled all the way. For his part, Jesse couldn't help teasing, "Well, your majesty, it's a fine thing for a queen to be walking through water on her own two feet!"

"Since I'm royalty, I can do it any way I like, and this is how I like it," she declared, feeling strong and capable.

They clambered over the side, each taking a place in the boat, Abigail and Katie front and center once again. "To Bethsaida," Abigail commanded, and obediently, Nahum and Daniel began rowing the boat across the water, to the place where the Savior had gone.

Once on shore, they all hiked up a grassy knoll to a beautiful field blanketed with blooming wildflowers of every hue. There they found a comfortable spot among the multitude that surrounded Jesus.

His disciples moved among the people, instructing them, "Please divide yourselves into groups of about fifty."

"Why do they want us to do that?" Jesse asked his father.

A man who stood close by answered, "They want to know just how many people are here. Most have followed Jesus all day and have not eaten. Jesus has instructed his disciples to feed us all, but I say it is impossible."

"Why is it impossible?" Katie asked him.

"They have only five loaves of bread and two fishes, and I heard that there are about five thousand people here. Five thousand, I tell you!" the man exclaimed.

Matthew heard the man with his ears, but his eyes were riveted on the Savior. He watched as

Jesus took the basket, which held but five loaves and two fishes. Looking toward heaven, Jesus blessed the contents of the basket. And then, although it was scarcely enough to feed five, He told the disciples to distribute the food to all five thousand.

The first group of fifty took a basket and passed it to one another. More baskets were passed to the next group, and to the next, until each person on the vast hillside had eaten.

"We have witnessed another miracle," Seth said to Matthew, as the two stood side by side, taking it all in. "Amazing, isn't it?"

"You know what amazes me?" Matthew said reverently. "Miracles show us Jesus' mighty power, but they also show how much He loves us."

"He *does* love us, doesn't He?" Seth said with feeling, watching his beloved daughter stand on her own to pass a basket full of fish.

And Matthew responded, "I guess now the important question is whether or not *we* love *Him* enough to obey."

Looking directly into Matthew's eyes, Seth asked, "What do you plan to tell your friend?"

"I am going to explain that I have promised to follow Jesus," Matthew replied with confidence. "I hope he understands why I can't help him cheat."

"Your light is shining already, my friend." Seth rested his hands on Matthew's shoulders.

Then, gazing up at Seth, Matthew asked, "And what have you decided to do?"

Seth smiled and replied, "My love for Jesus has also helped me choose the right. I have decided that my days collecting taxes are over. I am going to join my father in the fishing trade. I know in my heart that Jesus will help me."

"He will help both of us," Matthew said, throwing his arms around Seth. Then the man and the boy stood side by side for a moment, surveying the wondrous scene before them, their stomachs filled with food and their hearts filled with love.

Seth sat down among the multitude, and Abigail climbed into his lap. Seth motioned for Jesse to join them, and the three of them sat contentedly in the late afternoon sun, a truly happy family.

Katie, Matthew, and Peter sat behind them. "It makes me sad to know that we have to leave,"

Katie said quietly to her brothers. "But something tells me it's time to go home."

"Do we have to?" Peter moaned.

"It would be hard for Grandma to explain that her three grandchildren disappeared right from under her nose," Matthew said, chuckling at the thought.

"I guess you're right," Peter reluctantly agreed.

"We promised Abigail that we wouldn't leave without saying good-bye," Katie reminded her brothers, her eyes filling with tears.

"Oh, no, Katie! Don't do it. Do *not* cry," Matthew pleaded. "It only makes things harder."

Katie bravely tried to swallow her sniffles, and the three children approached Seth, Jesse, and Abigail. Abigail took one look at her friends and cried, "You're leaving, aren't you?" and tears welled up in her eyes, too.

"Please, no tears," Jesse instructed his sister, rolling his eyes. "Girls!" he groaned to Matthew, shaking his head.

But by this time, even Matthew was feeling a bit weepy.

"Are your parents coming for you?" Seth asked.

"No, but they'll be expecting us soon, so we must hurry," Katie explained, reaching out to hug Abigail.

"Matthew, thank you for removing your bushel basket," Seth said as they embraced tightly. "It has given me courage to get rid of my own. Whatever happens now, I will always carry the glow of your shining light in my heart."

"And I will carry yours," Matthew replied.

"Well, good-bye," Peter waved as he turned and loped away.

"We'd better hurry if we are going to catch him," Matthew said, grabbing Katie's hand and making a dash for Peter.

"Wait for us!" they called as they followed him over a small hill and into a grove of trees. Peter paused just long enough for them to catch up. Matthew used his free hand to grab Peter's, and with Katie holding the other, the three children felt the ground give way under their feet. And whoosh! Their journey home had begun.

Chapter Eleven

Home Again

When the wind stopped rushing around them, the children opened their eyes to find they were once more wearing normal clothes and nestled in pillows and blankets at Grandma's feet. And there she sat, just as they had left her, calmly reading from her Bible!

"And whithersoever he entered into villages, or cities, or country, they laid the sick in the streets, and besought him that they might touch if it were but the border of his garment: And as many as touched him were made whole." Slowly Grandma closed the book.

Katie quickly wiped away a tear. "That was a wonderful experience," she said. "I'm glad I was there."

Grandma lowered her glasses on her nose and peered down at Katie. Katie realized what she had said and quickly corrected herself, "Um, I mean, your painting is so real that it *seemed* like we were there."

"Well, thank you, Katie. I hoped you would get that feeling from my painting," Grandma winked. "Grab your journals and let's write down some of those feelings, shall we?"

The children opened their journals. "When Jesus lived on the earth, He performed many great miracles," Katie began writing. Then she looked up.

"Grandma, do miracles still happen today?" she asked, thinking of Abigail and Jairus's daughter and the baskets overflowing with bread and fish.

"All the time," Grandma said. "Every time a heart changes, the greatest miracle of all is at work."

"What's that, Grandma?" Peter asked.

"It is that Jesus came to earth and gave His life

for us so that we can repent and keep improving," Grandma answered. "Every time our heart chooses the right, we have experienced a small miracle."

"I think I've had that kind of miracle happen to me," Matthew said. "I was planning to make a wrong choice, but Jesus helped me feel His love, and now I want to follow Him more than anything."

"That's what Jesus meant when He said we should let our light shine!" Peter exclaimed, looking at his brother with pride.

"I wanted to hide mine under a bushel basket, didn't I?" Matthew smiled sheepishly at his little brother. "But Jesus changed all that today. You're right, Grandma. It *is* a miracle."

"Well, it sounds as though each of you has plenty to write." Grandma stood up. "I think I'll go in and fix our lunch. I have one more can of tuna fish. I'll bet I can make it stretch for four sandwiches."

"FISH?" Peter asked with his face screwed up into a grimace.

"Is there something wrong with fish?" Grandma asked.

"Oh, no," Matthew responded, digging his elbow into Peter's ribs.

"Ouch!" yelped Peter.

"We love fish," smiled Katie sweetly at Grandma.

"Wonderful! You keep writing. I'll be right back with our lunch." And with that, Grandma disappeared.

"You almost gave the whole thing away, Peter," Matthew scolded as soon as Grandma was out of earshot. "What were you thinking?"

"I'm sorry, but when she said 'fish,' I really lost it. Bread and fish twice in one day!" Peter moaned. "Besides, I think she knows where we've been."

"I'm not sure about that," Matthew replied. "And I don't want to tell her, in case she puts a stop to our adventures."

"She wouldn't do that, would she?" Peter sat straight up with a worried look on his face.

"Who wants to find out?" Katie asked him.

"Not me!" Peter declared.

"Me, neither," Katie said. "So I suggest you eat your whole sandwich without complaining!"

"Right, Sis," Peter saluted her ceremoniously.

"As long as those sandwiches don't keep multiplying," he added with an impish grin.

Peter and Katie opened their journals and began writing busily. Matthew leaned forward, thinking of how to come up with a good way to express all that had happened. As he leaned, he felt a jab in his jeans' pocket. Something hard and sharp was in there! Matthew reached in and drew out something that made him gasp with surprise.

"What is it, Matthew?" Katie asked.

Matthew wrapped his fingers around the small object. "Oh, it's nothing, Sis," Matthew replied, putting the object back into his hip pocket. And suddenly, he knew just what to write in his journal:

"Today, I brought home two souvenirs from my trip to the Galilee. The first is a feeling in my heart that I want to follow Jesus, no matter what. And the second is a little purple stone . . ."

About the Authors

Alice W. Johnson, a published author and composer, is a featured speaker for youth groups, adult firesides, and women's seminars. A former executive in a worldwide strategy consulting company, and then in a leadership training firm, Alice is now a homemaker living in Eagle, Idaho, with her husband and their four young children.

Allison H. Warner gained her early experience living with her family in countries around the world. Returning to the United States as a young woman, she began her vocation as an actress and writer, developing and performing in such productions as *The Farley Family Reunion.* She and her husband reside in Provo, Utah, where they are raising two active boys.

About the Illustrator

Jerry Harston holds a degree in graphic design and has illustrated more than thirty children's books. He has received many honors for his art, and his clients include numerous Fortune 500 corporations. Jerry and his wife, Libby, live in Sandy, Utah. Their six children and sixteen grandchildren serve as excellent critics for his illustrations.